THE HAUNTED!

HAUNTED HOTELS

A Crabtree Branches Book

THOMAS KINGSLEY TROUPE

CRABTREE
Publishing Company
www.crabtreebooks.com

School-to-Home Support for Caregivers and Teachers

This high-interest book is designed to motivate striving students with engaging topics while building fluency, vocabulary, and an interest in reading. Here are a few questions and activities to help the reader build upon his or her comprehension skills.

Before Reading:

- *What do I think this book is about?*
- *What do I know about this topic?*
- *What do I want to learn about this topic?*
- *Why am I reading this book?*

During Reading:

- *I wonder why...*
- *I'm curious to know...*
- *How is this like something I already know?*
- *What have I learned so far?*

After Reading:

- *What was the author trying to teach me?*
- *What are some details?*
- *How did the photographs and captions help me understand more?*
- *Read the book again and look for the vocabulary words.*
- *What questions do I still have?*

Extension Activities:

- *What was your favorite part of the book? Write a paragraph on it.*
- *Draw a picture of your favorite thing you learned from the book.*

TABLE OF CONTENTS

CHECKING IN... FOREVER

You awaken in the middle of the night and sit up. It feels like someone is watching you. The air is cold, making you shiver. In the darkness, you see a figure standing at the end of the bed. Your heart races as you turn on the bedside lamp. As soon as the room is lit up, the figure is gone. Is this hotel actually haunted?

Every state or country has a haunted history. Hotels are where travelers check in for a relaxing vacation. Unfortunately, some of the ghostly guests from long ago never bothered to check out! For now, the hotels in this book are still open for business, haunted or not!

Grab your flashlight and take a deep breath. You're about to discover why these hotels are among...

THE HAUNTED.

FRIGHTENING FACT

There is at least one haunted hotel in every state in the United States of America.

HOLLYWOOD ROOSEVELT HOTEL

Along the Hollywood Walk of Fame in California sits the Hollywood Roosevelt Hotel. The Roosevelt opened in 1927 and many famous guests have stayed there.

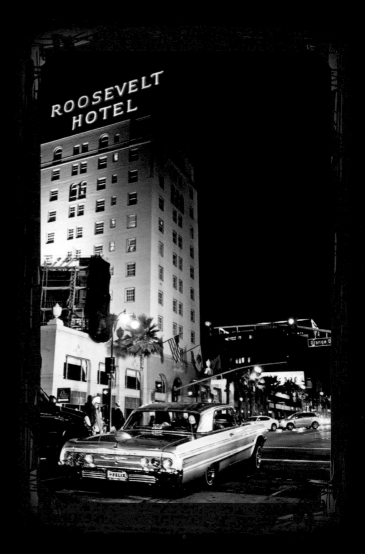

Some claim to have seen the ghosts of famous actors. Marilyn Monroe's image often appears in a mirror in room 1200 where she lived for two years. Montgomery Clift's ghost is said to pat visitors on the shoulder.

FRIGHTENING FACT

Famous people aren't the only ghosts that haunt the Roosevelt. Some have witnessed a ghostly girl in a blue dress. The little girl is known as Caroline and seems to be looking for her mother.

ANCIENT RAM INN, ENGLAND

The Ancient Ram Inn in England was built in 1145. It was the former home of a priest and rumored to sit on top of an ancient **pagan** burial ground.

Evil things happened in the inn's past. A woman who was believed to be a witch hid inside Ancient Ram. She was later captured and burned at the stake.

FRIGHTENING FACT

One visitor was said to have been lifted and thrown across the hall in the Bishop's Room of the Ancient Ram Inn.

A man named John Humphries bought the inn in 1968 and decided to make it his home. He claimed that during his first night's sleep, a **demonic** force grabbed his arm. It pulled him from his bed and dragged him across the room.

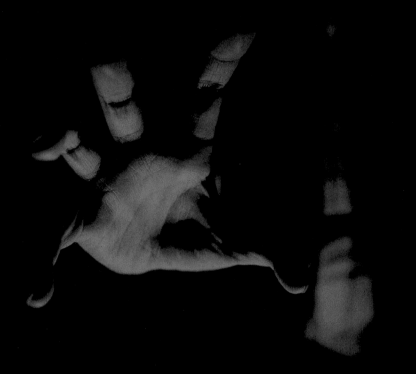

John was determined to live in the haunted inn. His wife and three daughters didn't want anything to do with it. They left, but John lived at the inn for almost 50 years.

Broken daggers and small skeletons were found buried beneath a staircase at Ancient Ram Inn. The **remains** appeared to be the bones of children. The daggers were likely used for some sort of dark ritual or sacrifice.

LA FONDA
ON THE PLAZA, NEW MEXICO

In New Mexico stands the hotel known as La Fonda on the Plaza. Built in 1922, it sits on the site of Santa Fe's first inn, back when the city was established around 1607.

Guests have seen the ghost of a young bride who was murdered on her wedding night. Others have seen the **specter** of a cowboy hanging around the bar.

One of the most common **paranormal** occurrences is the appearance of Chief Justice John P. Slough's ghost. He was shot to death in the lobby in 1867. Visitors have heard Judge Slough's footsteps as he walks the hotel hallways. Others have spotted him wearing his favorite long, black coat before he disappears!

BORGVATTNET VICARAGE
RAGUNDA, SWEDEN

The Borgvattnet Vicarage is one of Sweden's most haunted locations. It was built in 1876 as a home for **vicars**. From the outside, it looks like an old, wooden cabin at the edge of the woods.

Sometime in 1927, reports of hauntings came from the vicarage. The vicar living there claimed his laundry was torn from the clothesline without explanation.

Nearly every vicar and family member that moved into the house since has witnessed paranormal activity. Some have seen things move on their own. Others have heard screams. Shadow people have appeared.

The vicarage is no longer a home for holy people. It is now a bed and breakfast for any brave soul who wants to spend the night.

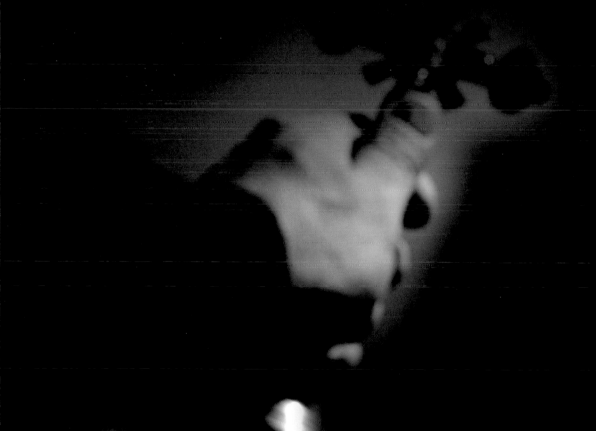

FRIGHTENING FACT

In the early 1980s, Father Tore Forslund vowed to rid the vicarage of ghosts. Nothing changed and he left within a year's time.

RED LION INN, MASSACHUSETTS

Travelers who want a good night's sleep should probably avoid The Red Lion Inn. Built in 1773, this haunted hotel is located in Stockbridge, Massachusetts.

The fourth floor seems to be the spookiest. People have reported seeing a ghostly girl carrying flowers. A man in a top hat likes to stand over the bed of sleeping guests.

FAIRMONT BANFF SPRINGS HOTEL

The Fairmont Banff Springs Hotel in Calgary, resembles a castle nestled in the Canadian mountainside. It opened in 1888 and quickly became popular for both the living and the dead.

Several ghosts haunt the massive hotel, including a bride who fell to her death on a stone staircase. A **bellman** named Sam is believed to help guests with their luggage and unlock doors.

Rumor has it that a family was murdered in room 873. Some guests who have stayed in the room since have been awoken by screaming. Bloody handprints were said to appear on the mirrors. Visit the hotel now and you'll find that room 873 is no longer there. Many believe it was closed up to keep visitors out!

SAVOY HOTEL, MUSSOORIE, INDIA

In Mussoorie, India, sits the beautiful Savoy Hotel, built in 1902. Despite looking like a peaceful resort, the large property has a haunted history.

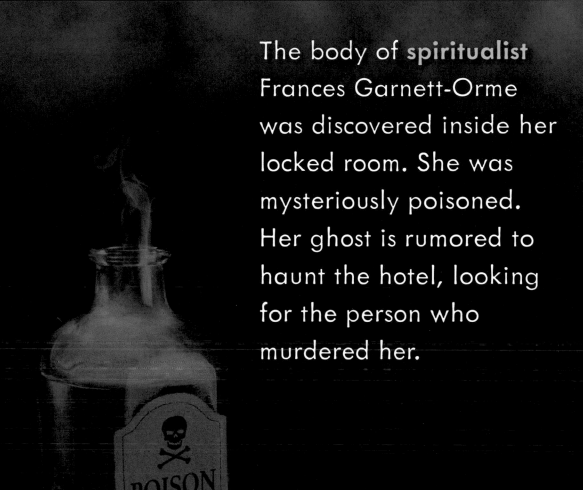

The body of **spiritualist** Frances Garnett-Orme was discovered inside her locked room. She was mysteriously poisoned. Her ghost is rumored to haunt the hotel, looking for the person who murdered her.

FRIGHTENING FACT

A number of classic authors were interested in the case of Lady Garnett, including Sherlock Holmes, author Sir Arthur Conan Doyle, and mystery writer Agatha Christie.

THE STANLEY HOTEL

Perhaps one of the most popular haunted hotels is the Stanley Hotel in Estes Park, Colorado. It opened in 1909 and sits near the entrance of Rocky Mountain National Park.

The hotel was built by and named after F.O. Stanley, the man who invented the Stanley Steemer Automobile. He passed away in 1940, but according to many, he never left the hotel behind.

F. O. Stanley

Mr. Stanley's ghost is thought to sometimes appear to guests near the reception desk. The phantom of his wife Flora often plays the piano in an otherwise empty music room.

Elizabeth was a **chambermaid** who nearly died in an explosion at the Stanley in the 1920s. She recovered and worked there until she died at age 90. Her ghost passes through doors to straighten up the rooms.

The Stanley Hotel is also famous for being the **inspiration** for horror novelist Stephen King. He and his wife Tabitha, also a novelist, stayed there in 1974. After a nightmare, he woke up and came up with the idea for his best-selling novel *The Shining*. A movie based on the book features the ghosts of two young girls (above right).

CONCLUSION

Are there really ghosts staying in the same hotels as the living? What one person sees, another might explain away.

It's up to you to decide for yourself. If you hear or see something creepy, write it down or capture it with a camera. The evidence you discover might bring us closer to understanding...THE HAUNTED.

GLOSSARY

bellman (BEL-muhn): A person who works in a hotel and brings luggage to guests' rooms

chambermaid (CHAYM-bur-mayd): A maid who cleans and takes care of bedrooms in a hotel

demonic (di-MON-ik): An evil spirit, something that wishes to cause harm

inspiration (in-spihr-AY-shuhn): Something that causes someone to act, create, or feel emotions

pagan (PAY-guhn): A religion that focuses on spirituality or nature

paranormal (pa-ruh-NOR-muhl): Strange events that are beyond normal understanding

remains (ri-MAYNZ): The body of a dead person

specter (SPEK-tur): Another word for ghost

spiritualist (SPIHR-i-tyool-ist): A person who believes the spirits of the dead can communicate with living people

vicars (VI-kurz): Ministers in charge of churches who represent other ministers

INDEX

WEBSITES TO VISIT

https://kids.kiddle.co/Ghost

www.hauntedrooms.co.uk/ghost-
stories-kids-scary-childrens

www.ghostsandgravestones.com/
how-to-ghost-hunt

ABOUT THE AUTHOR

Thomas Kingsley Troupe

Thomas Kingsley Troupe is the author of a whole pile of books for kids. He's written about ghosts, Bigfoot, werewolves, and even a book about dirt. When he's not writing or reading, he investigates the paranormal as part of the Twin Cities Paranormal Society. He lives in Woodbury, Minnesota with his 2 sons.

CRABTREE Publishing Company

Produced by: Blue Door Education for Crabtree Publishing
Written by: Thomas Kingsley Troupe
Designed by: Jennifer Dydyk
Edited by: Kelli Hicks
Proofreader: Crystal Sikkens

The images/photos depicting "ghosts" in this book are artists' interpretations. The publisher does not claim these are actual images/photos taken of the ghosts mentioned in this book.

Cover: Man and hotel © Ollyy, skull on cover and throughout book © Fer Gregory, pages 4-5 creepy picture borders here and throughout book © Dmitry Natashin, page 4 © feeling lucky, page 5 hotel © Gudmund, page 6 © Andrey Bayda, page 7 Marilyn © Editorial credit: Javi Az / Shutterstock.com, hotel interior © Editorial credit: littlenySTOCK / Shutterstock.com, pages 8-9 © Anneka, page 10 © feeling lucky, page 11 © Masarik, page 12 © Andriy Blokhin, page 13 ghost bride © Salome Hoogendijk, page 14-15 © Jojoo64, page 16 © jirakit suparatanameta, page 17 © itsmejust, page 20 © Paula Cobleigh, page 21 bell-hop © Pressmaster, handprint © Kirill Kurashov, page 23 © ADragan, pages 24-25 © MHalvorson, page 26 © Kaul Photo and Cinema, page 27 Stephen King © Editorial credit: Everett Collection / Shutterstock.com, Twins from movie The Shining © Hethers, page 28 © Cinemato, page 29 © feeling lucky. All images from Shutterstock.com except page 8 © Brian Robert Marshall / Ram Inn, Potters Pond, Wotton under Edge / CC BY-SA 2.0, page 13 John Potts Slough public domain image, Page 18 Red Lion Inn, Massachusetts © John Phelan https://creativecommons.org/licenses/by-sa/4.0/deed.en, page 19 © ysbrandcosijn/istockphoto.com, page 22 Nick Kenrick/Flickr https://creativecommons.org/licenses/by/2.0/ ,

Library and Archives Canada Cataloguing in Publication
Title: Haunted hotels / Thomas Kingsley Troupe.
Names: Troupe, Thomas Kingsley, author.
Description: Series statement: The haunted! |
   "A Crabtree branches book". | Includes index.
Identifiers: Canadiana (print) 20210220201 |
   Canadiana (ebook) 2021022021X |
   ISBN 9781427155566 (hardcover) |
   ISBN 9781427155627 (softcover) |
   ISBN 9781427155689 (HTML) |
   ISBN 9781427155740 (EPUB) |
   ISBN 9781427155801 (read-along ebook)
Subjects: LCSH: Haunted hotels—Juvenile literature. |
   LCSH: Ghosts—Juvenile literature.
Classification: LCC BF1474.5 .T76 2022 | DDC j133.1/22—dc23

Library of Congress Cataloging-in-Publication Data
Names: Troupe, Thomas Kingsley, author.
Title: Haunted hotels / Thomas Kingsley Troupe.
Description: New York, NY : Crabtree Publishing Company, [2022] |
   Series: The haunted! - a Crabtree Branches book | Includes index.
Identifiers: LCCN 2021022534 (print) |
   LCCN 2021022535 (ebook) |
   ISBN 9781427155566 (hardcover) |
   ISBN 9781427155627 (paperback) |
   ISBN 9781427155689 (ebook) |
   ISBN 9781427155740 (epub) |
   ISBN 9781427155801
Subjects: LCSH: Haunted hotels--Juvenile literature. | Ghosts--Juvenile literature.
Classification: LCC BF1474.5 .T76 2022 (print) | LCC BF1474.5 (ebook) |
   DDC 133.1/22--dc23
LC record available at https://lccn.loc.gov/2021022534
LC ebook record available at https://lccn.loc.gov/2021022535

Crabtree Publishing Company

www.crabtreebooks.com   1-800-387-7650

Printed in the U.S.A./072021/CG20210514

Copyright © 2022 **CRABTREE PUBLISHING COMPANY**

Published in the United States
Crabtree Publishing
347 Fifth Avenue, Suite 1402-145
New York, NY, 10016

Published in Canada
Crabtree Publishing
616 Welland Ave.
St. Catharines, ON, L2M 5V6